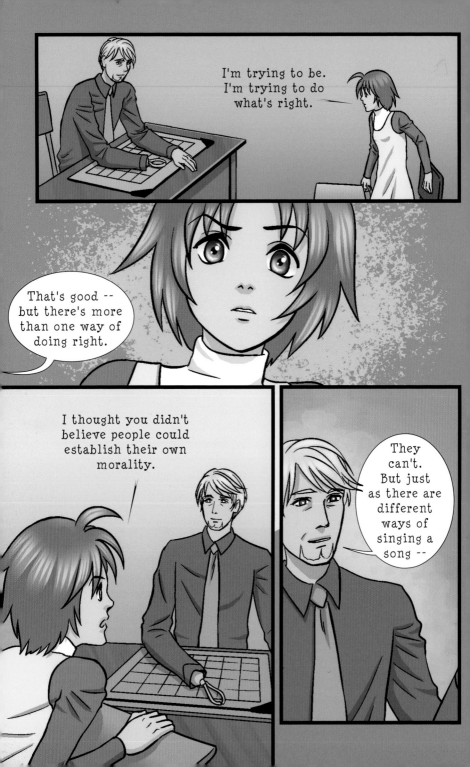

Hi, Mom!

You went shopping?

Un-huh. Just at the thrift shop.

You might say I'm looking for a new look.

Hi, Dad!

Hi, Kimberly.

You're only wearing this around the house, right?

Of course, Dad! These aren't **school clothes!**

Elsewhere, however...

I was checking about booking the arcade for a youth group party.

...oh...

...uh...aren't you going to say anything?

Do I have to ?

...no...

PARADISE

FRAULEIN STEIN'S
MONSTER

KIMBERLY
CALVIN

EDDIE
BRADFORD

SERENITY
HARPER

WRITTEN.PRODUCED.DIRECTED
BY
TIM PATTERSON

Fraulein Stein's MONSTER

BASED ON THE NOVEL
FRANKENSTEIN BY MARY
WOLLSTONECRAFT SHELLEY
AND THE 1910 FILM
FRANKENSTEIN
WRITTEN AND DIRECTED BY
J. SEARLE DAWLEY

KIMBERLY CALVIN
as Fraulein Elsbeth Stein

DEREK ANGSTROM
as Viktor

TIM PATTERSON
as The Burgomeister

LORI MARTIN
as The Professor

SERENITY HARPER
as The Monster

EDDIE BRADFORD
as Dr. Eccles

SALLY RICHMOND
as Agatha

It's a beautiful Sabbath, darling. You should rest from your studies.

I can't. I'm determined to discover the secret of creating life.

'Tis no secret. I'll show you once we are wed.

I don't mean that old fashioned way!

This is the 18th century--a modern age!

Fraulein Stein, may I see you? I have heard of your research.

I make no effort to hide it.

Perhaps you should.

Why? Because I dare challenge God's supremacy?

I need to learn more! His journals come so tantalizingly close, but they don't reveal the truth!

Why don't you ask him?

He was born 98 years ago. He must be dead.

Do you know that for a fact?

Transylvania?!?!? Why go there?

We were to be wed upon your graduation.

I have not finished my studies.

When will you finish?

Soon...

...I hope...

Years ago he locked himself away in his tower. No one has seen him since!

Surely someone must have gone to his tower.

Never! Dr. Eccles may be dead, but his servants live on!

They maintain the tower--and his secrets.

Then I shall seek them!

BANG BANG BANG

CREEEEEAK

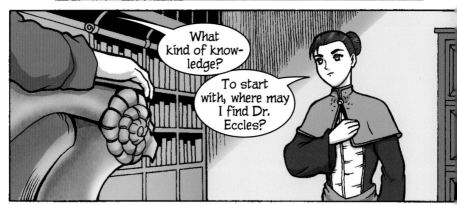

My dear, you are speaking to him.

Now again I ask: What do you want?

The secret of creating life!

And you believe I possess it?

I believe you have come closer than anyone.

And what would you give for this secret--?

--or the part of it I possess?

Any-thing you desire!

Careful, girl! I desire quite a lot.

Agreed.

Mojo, prepare the chambers adjoining mine. Jomo, fetch her bags.

We shall begin tonight. No time like the present, especially at my age...

You will be served, Herr Doktor...

Your master is dead.

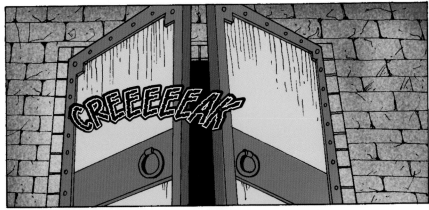

What are you doing here?

Wondering why you aren't overjoyed to see your fiance!

You come at a bad time.

There never seems to be any time now.

Please, Viktor, be understanding. I cannot entertain you at this juncture.

Very well.

I shall return to the village and leave with the morning carriage.

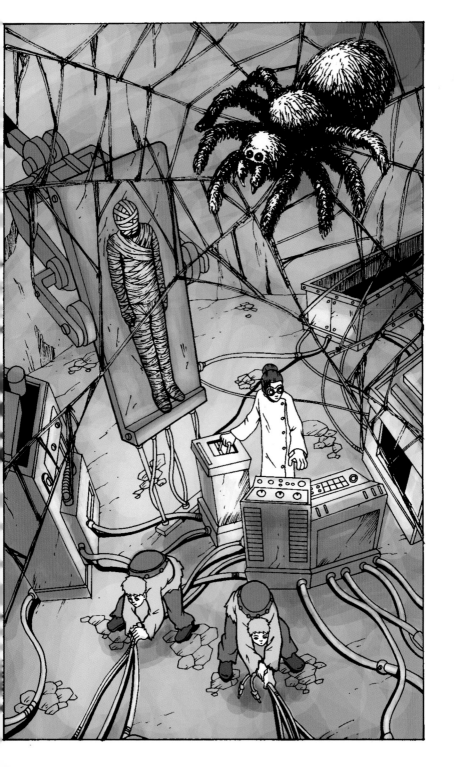

RAP RAP RAP

"?"

Take me away from here!

Darling, what happened?

INN

Please don't make me tell you! Promise you'll never ask again!

Darling, are you ready?

Viktor!

Stay behind this until I can send him away!

It's bad luck to see a bride before the wedding.

You, superstitious?

Is everything all right? You look troubled.

It's... it's nothing...

After we are married, you need never be troubled again!

UNGH!

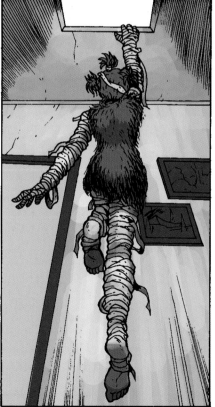

Its been hours and we have found no trace of this criminal.

She's close by--I can feel it!

It is useless. Come, let us return.

No! I must destroy her!

You carry your thirst for revenge too far.

Not revenge but... responsibility.

Very well—stay at yo own peril

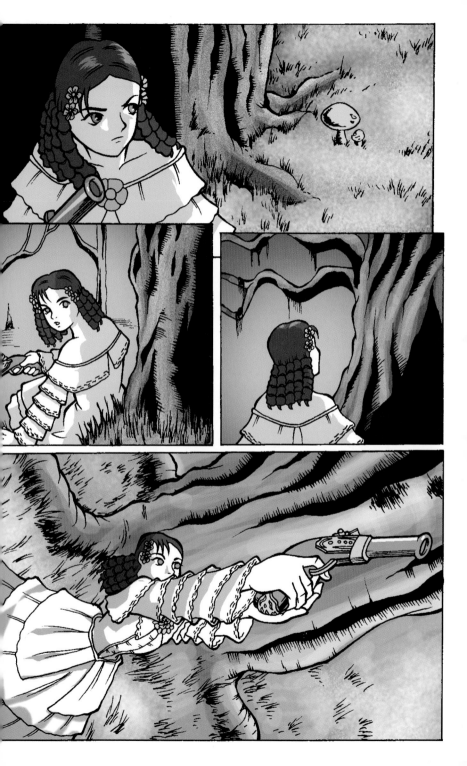

How We Made

"FRAULEIN STEIN'S MONSTER"

by

Serenity Harper (Class 6a)

[margin note: Only one exclamaition point!]

NO FAIR!!! A queen one month, a monster the next! And I know Kimberly was laffing at me all the time! *[correction: laughing]*

Anywho, I was the monster, K. was the mad scientist. It was kinda fun 'cuz in *[corrections: kind of / because]* too many horror films the girls just stand there and scream (if not worse) and this time we got to make stuff happen. Woo-hoo!!! GURL POWER!!! *[correction: GIRL]*

So Tim tells me what I'm supposed to wear and I'm like it's gonna take 4ever to *[corrections: going to / forever]* get all wrapped up like that and Eddie says I'll help (in your dreams, Eddie!) but I said thanx but no thanx (now Derek, on the other hand...). *[correction: thanks]*

So I ask Lori if she can help and she got kinda weird and said no then Sally *[correction: kind of]* had this really great idea which is we got an old set of her bro's jammies and we *[correction: was]* sewed the bandages to them so instead of getting wrapped up all the time I could slip the costume on and off real EZ. *[correction: easy]*

And that big crowd scene with the torches and pitchforks? It was only six people! We made cutouts of rows and rows of pitchforks and torches, then we crouched down and waved them in front of the camera while Tim and K. were talking and when we were done you'd think there were a 100 people in the scene (Tim says it was a LOT easier than trying to add us all digitally again).

SPOILER: K. goes nutz and gets locked up in an insane asylum at the end. I wish..."Nuts" is not a polite term for mentally disabled people.

C-ya!

[margin note: C-ren Congratulations! You passed! No summer school for you! See you next fall!]

We heard the call...

Hey!
Serenity ™
Where did
you go
?!?!?

...and here she is!

Refreshed art!

Restored dialog!

Brand new covers!

Same ol' Serenity!

Don't miss any of her
new re-releases from
Thomas Nelson!
"Bad Girl In Town"
"Stepping Out"
"Basket Case"
"Rave and Rant"
"Snow Biz"
"You Shall Love..."

Find her
=oof!=
in stores
=grunt!=
now!

I sure
hope her
books
aren't
this
heavy!

Don't worry,
they're light
reading...

IT'S

LIFE !
CAMERA !
ACTION !

starring

Serenity™

Serenity is back with
ALL NEW STORIES
that mix humor, heartache,
homework & just a touch of
Hollywood hoopla as she
and her friends start
making their own brand of
off-beat movies !

ALL THE SASS & TWICE THE FUN!

Don't miss these great new
titles from Thomas Nelson
& Realbuzz Studios !

"Space Cadet vs. Drama Queen"
"Sunday Best"
"Choosing Change"
"Girl Overboard"

MAKE THE JUMP TO OUR WEBSITES!

www.SerenityBuzz.com
www.GoofyfootGurl.com
and
www.RealbuzzStudios.com not only talk about
Serenity and the Prayer Club but also upcoming new
series from Thomas Nelson and Realbuzz Studios like
GOOFYFOOT GURL and many, many more!

Make sure you visit us regularly
for advance news, fun facts, downloads, contests
and challenges, as well as online shopping!

Can you make a video?
Do you have a recipe?

Exciting new contests
coming soon to
www.RealbuzzStudios.com!

Looking For

Serenity™ Swag

Or

Goofyfoot™ Gear ?

Check out our online shop at
www.RealbuzzStudios.com
www.SerenityBuzz.com
www.GoofyfootGurl.com
www.GoofyfootGuy.com
[Protoypes shown; final product may differ slightly.]

Serenity

Created by Realbuzz Studios, Inc.
Min Kwon, Primary Artist

Serenity throws a big wet sloppy one out to:
Sarah White, pinch hitter extraordinaire!

SMACK!
Luv Ya !!!

©&TM 2007 by Realbuzz Studios   ISBN 1-59554-397-X / 978-1-59554-397-

www.RealbuzzStudios.com
www.SerenityBuzz.com

Published by Thomas Nelson, Inc. Nashville, TN 37214 www.thomasnelson.com

Library of Congress Cataloguing-in-Publication Data
Applied For

Scripture quotations marked NCV are taken from
The HOLY BIBLE, New Century VERSION®. NCV®.
Copyright © 2001 by Nelson Bibles.
Used by permission of Thomas Nelson. All rights reserved.

Printed in Singapore.
5 4 3 2 1